A MASQUE OF MERCY

BY

ROBERT FROST

HENRY HOLT AND COMPANY

NEW YORK

PRINTED IN THE UNITED STATES OF AMERICA

CHARACTERS

My Brother's Keeper
Jesse Bel, his wife
Paul, a doctor
Jonas Dove, a fugitive

A MASQUE OF MERCY

A bookstore late at night. The Keeper's wife
Pulls down the window curtain on the door
And locks the door. One customer, locked in,
Stays talking with the Keeper at a show case.
The Keeper's wife has hardly turned away
Before the door's so violently tried
It makes her move as if to reinforce it.

Jesse Bel   You can't come in! (*Knock, knock*) The store is closed!

Paul   Late, late, too late, you cannot enter now.

Jesse Bel   We can't be always selling people things.
He doesn't go.

Keeper   You needn't be so stern.
Open enough to find out who it is.

Jesse Bel   Keeper, you come and see. Or you come, Paul.
Our second second-childhood case tonight.

[1]

Where do these senile runaways escape from?
Wretchedness in a stranger frightens me
More than it touches me.

Paul   You may come in.

Fugitive   (*Entering hatless in a whirl of snow*)
God's after me!

Jesse Bel   You mean the Devil is.

Fugitive   No, God.

Jesse Bel   I never heard of such a thing.

Fugitive   Haven't you heard of Thompson's Hound of Heaven?

Paul   "I fled Him, down the nights and down the days;
I fled Him, down the arches of the years."

Keeper   This is a bookstore—not a sanctuary.

Jesse Bel   I thought you just now said it was a gift shop.

Keeper   Don't you be bitter about it. I'm not bitter.

Fugitive   Well, I could use a book.

[2]

Keeper	What book?

Fugitive	A Bible.

Keeper   To find out how to get away from God?
Which is what people use it for too often—
And why we wouldn't have one in the store.
We don't believe the common man should read it.
Let him seek his religion in the Church.

Jesse Bel   Keeper, be still. Pay no attention to him.
He's being a religious snob for fun.
The name his mother gave him is to blame
For Keeper's levity: My Brother's Keeper.
She didn't do it to him to be quaint,
But out of politics. She told me so.
She was left over from the Brook Farm venture.

Keeper   Why is God after you?—to save your soul?

Fugitive   No, make me prophesy.

Jesse Bel   And—you—just—won't?

Fugitive   Haven't you noticed anything (hear that!)
Since I came in?

[3]

Keeper   Hear what? That army truck?

Fugitive   Look, I don't need the Bible to consult.
             I just thought if you had a copy handy,
             I could point out my sort of passport in it.
             There is a story you may have forgotten
             About a whale.

Keeper   Oh, you mean Moby Dick
             By Rockwell Kent that everybody's reading.
             Trust me to help you find the book you want.

Jesse Bel Keeper, be still. He knows what book he wants.
             He said the Bible.

Fugitive   I should hate to scare you
             With the suspicion at this hour of night
             That I might be a confidence impostor.
             I'm Jonas Dove—if that is any help.

Paul   Which is the same as saying Jonah, Jonah—
             Ah, Jonah, Jonah—twice—reproachfully.

Fugitive   Spare me the setting of my fate to music.
             How did you know that way to break my heart?
             Who are you?

                              [4]

Paul   Who are you?

Jonah   I think you know,
          You seem so ready at translating names.
          Unless I'm much mistaken in myself
          This is the seventh time I have been sent
          To prophesy against the city evil.

Keeper   What have you got against the city?

Jonah   *He* knows.
          We have enough against it, haven't we?
          Cursed be the era that congested it.

Keeper   Come, come, you talk like an agrarian.
          The city is all right. To live in one
          Is to be civilized, stay up and read
          Or sing and dance all night and see sunrise
          By waiting up instead of getting up.
          The country's only useful as a place
          To rest at times from being civilized.
          You take us two, we're losers in this store,
          So losers in the city, but we're game:
          We don't go back on grapes we couldn't reach.
          We blame ourselves. We're good sports, aren't we, Bel?

Jesse Bel   I'm not a sport and don't pretend I am one.
It's only fair to Keeper to inform you
His favorite reading is seed catalogues.
When he gets too agrarian for me
I take to drink—at least I take *a* drink.

(*She has her own glass in a vacant chair*)

Paul   She'll take to drink and see how we like that.

Keeper   Bel is a solitary social drinker.
She doesn't mind not offering a drink
To anyone around when she is drinking.

Jesse Bel   We're poor—that's why. My man can't earn a living.

Keeper   Is it just any city you're against?

Jonah   Yes, but New York will do as an example.

Keeper   Well, you're as good as in New York this minute—
Or bad as in New York.

Jonah   I know I am.
That was where my engagement was to speak
This very night. I had the hall all hired,
The audience assembled. There I was

[6]

Behind the scenes ordained and advertised
To prophesy, and full of prophecy,
Yet could not bring myself to say a word.
I left light shining on an empty stage
And fled to you. But you receive me not.

Keeper   Yes we do too, with sympathy my friend.
Your righteous indignation fizzled out,
Or else you were afraid of being mobbed
If what you had to say was disagreeable.

Jesse Bel   Your courage failed. The saddest thing in life
Is that the best thing in it should be courage.
Them is my sentiments, and Mr. Flood,
Since you propose it, I believe I will.

Jonah   Please, someone understand.

Paul   I understand.

Jonah   These others don't.

Paul   You don't yourself entirely.

Jonah   What don't I understand? It's easy enough.
I'm in the Bible, all done out in story.
I've lost my faith in God to carry out

[7]

The threats He makes against the city evil.
I can't trust God to be unmerciful.

Keeper   You've lost your faith in God? How wicked of you.

Jesse Bel   You naughty kitten, you shall have no pie.

Paul   Keeper's the kind of Unitarian
Who having by elimination got
From many gods to Three and Three to One,
Thinks why not taper off to none at all,
Except as father putative to sort of
Legitimize the brotherhood of man,
So we can hang together in a strike.

Keeper   Now we are hearing from the Exegete.
You don't know Paul: he's in the Bible too.
He is the fellow who theologized
Christ almost out of Christianity.
Look out for him.

Paul   "Look out for me" is right.
I'm going to tell you something, Jonas Dove.
I'm going to take the nonsense out of you
And give you rest, poor Wandering Jew.

Jonah   I'm not

[8]

The Wandering Jew—I'm who I say I am,
A prophet with the Bible for credentials.

Paul   I never said you weren't. I recognized you.
You are the universal fugitive,
Escapist as we say, though you are not
Running away from Him you think you are
But from His mercy-justice contradiction.
Mercy and justice are a contradiction.
But here's where your evasion has an end.
I have to tell you something that will spoil
Indulgence in your form of melancholy
Once and for all. I'm going to make you see
How relatively little justice matters.

Jonah   I see what you are up to: robbing me
Of my incentive—canceling my mission.

Paul   I am empowered to excuse you from it.

Jonah   You! Who are you? I asked you once before.

Jesse Bel   He is our analyst.

Jonah   Your analyst?

Keeper   Who keeps our bookstore annals.

[9]

Jesse Bel　　　　　　　　　　　　　　Stop it, Keeper.

An analyst's the latest thing in doctors.

He's mine. That's what he is (you asked)—my doctor.

I'm sick.

Jonah　　　　　　Of what?

Jesse Bel　　　　　　　　　　　　Oh, everything I guess.

The doctors say the trouble with me is

I'm not in love. I didn't love the doctor

I had before. That's why I changed to Paul—

To try another.

Paul　　　　　　　　　　　　Jesse Bel's a girl

Whose cure will lie in getting her idea

Of the word love corrected. She got off

To a bad start it seems in the wrong school

Of therapy.

Jesse Bel　　　　　　　　I don't love Paul—as yet.

Jonah　　How about loving God?

Jesse Bel　　　　　　　　　　　You make me shrug.

And I don't love you either, do I, Keeper?

Keeper   Don't lay your hand on me to say it, shameless.
Let me alone.

Jesse Bel   I'm sick. Joe's sick. The world's sick.
I'll take to drink—at least I'll take *a* drink.

Jonah   My name's not Joe. I don't like what she says.
It's Greenwich Village cocktail party talk—
Big-city talk. I'm getting out of here.
I'm—bound—away. (*He quotes it to the tune*)

Paul   Oh no, you're not. You're staying here tonight.
You locked the door, Bel. Let me have the key.

(*He goes and takes it from the door himself*)

Jonah   Then I'm a prisoner?

Paul   You are tonight.
We take it you were sent in here for help.
And help you're going to get.

Jonah   I'll break your door down.
Always the same when I set out in flight.
I take the first boat. God puts up a storm
That someone in the crew connects with me.
The sailors throw me overboard for luck,

[11]

Or as you might say throw me to the whale—
For me to disagree with him and get spit out
Right back in the same trouble I was in.
You're modern; so the whale you throw me to
Will be some soulless lunatic asylum—
For me to disagree with any science
There may be there and get spit out again.

Jesse Bel   You poor, poor swallowable little man.

Paul   If you would take the hands out of your hair
And calm yourself. Be sane! I hereby hold
Your forearms in the figure of a cross
The way it rested two points on the ground
At every station but the final one.

Jonah   What good is that?

Paul   I'll make you see what good.

Jonah   I *am* sick as she says. Nothing exhausts me
Like working myself up to prophesy
And then not prophesying. (*He sits down*)

Jesse Bel   Can you interpret dreams? I dreamed last night
Someone took curved nail scissors and snipped off
My eyelids so I couldn't shut my eyes

[12]

To anything that happened any more.

Jonah   She's had some loss she can't accept from God—
Is that it? Some Utopian belief—
Or child, and this is motherly resentment?

Jesse Bel   You look so sleepless. If he'd promise us
To go straight home. We wouldn't keep him, would we?
Where are you staying—anywhere in town?

Jonah   Under the bandstand in Suburban Park.

Jesse Bel   Why, what a story. At this time of year
There's not a footprint to it in the snow.

Paul   Jonah, I'm glad, not sad to hear you say
You can't trust God to be unmerciful.
There you have the beginning of all wisdom.

Keeper   One minute, may I Paul?—before we leave
Religion for these philosophic matters.
That's the right style of coat for prophecy
You're sporting there. I'll bet you're good at it.
Shall it be told we had a prophet captive
And let him get off without prophesying?
Let's have some prophecy. What form of ruin
(For ruin I assume was what it was)

[13]

Had you in mind to visit on the city,
Rebellion, pestilence, invasion?

Jonah   Earthquake
Was what I thought of.

Keeper   Have you any grounds,
Or undergrounds, for confidence in earthquake?

Jonah   It's good geology—the Funday Fault,
A fracture in the rocks beneath New York
That only needs a finger touch from God
To spring it like a deadfall and the fault
In nature would wipe out all human fault.
(*He stops to listen*) That's a mighty storm,
And we are shaken. But it isn't earthquake.
Another possibility I thought of—

(*He stops to listen and his unspoken thought,*
Projected from the lantern of his eyes,
Is thrown in script as at Belshazzar's feast
On the blank curtain on the outer door)

—Was Babel: everyone developing
A language of his own to write his book in,
And one to cap the climax by combining
All language in a one-man tongue-confusion.

(*He starts to speak, but stops again to listen.*
The writing on the screen must change too fast
For any but the rapidest eye readers)

[14]

Suspicion of the income-tax returns,
A question who was getting the most out
Of business, might increase into a madness.
The mob might hold a man up in the streets
And tear his clothes off to examine him
To find if there were pockets in his skin
As in a smuggler's at the diamond fields,
Where he was hoarding more than they enjoyed.

Paul   We can all see what's passing in your mind.
(I won't have Keeper calling it religion.)
It's a hard case. It's got so prophecy
Is a disease of your imagination.
You're so lost in the virtuosity
Of getting up good ruins, you've forgotten
What the sins are men ought to perish for.

Jonah   You wrong me.

Keeper   Well then, name a single sin.

Jonah   Another possibility I thought of—

Jesse Bel   There he goes off into another trance.

Keeper   You stick to earthquake, you have something there—
Something we'll know we're getting when we get it.

[15]

Paul   (*Taking a walk off down the store distressed*)
         Keeper, I'll turn on you if you keep on.

Keeper   If I were in your place though, Mr. Prophet,
         I'd *want* to be more certain I was called
         Before I undertook so delicate
         A mission as to have to tell New York
         'Twas in for an old-fashioned shaking down
         Like the one Joshua gave Jerico.
         You wouldn't want the night clubs laughing at you.

Jesse Bel Or THE NEW YORKER.

Keeper   When was the last time
         You heard from God—I mean had orders from Him?

Jonah   I'm hearing from Him now, did you but notice.
         Don't any of you hear a sound?

Keeper   The storm!
         Merely the windows rattling in the storm.
         Trucks going by to war. A war is on.

Jonah   That is no window. That's a show case rattling.
         That is your antiques rattling on a shelf.

Jesse Bel You're doing it.

[16]

| Jonah | I'm not. How could I be? |

| Jesse Bel | You're doing something to our minds. |

| Jonah | I'm not. |
| | Don't *you* feel something? |

| Paul | Leave me out of this. |

(*He leans away in tolerant distaste*)

Jonah	And here come all your Great Books tumbling down!
	You see the Lord God is a jealous God!
	He wrote one book. Let there be no more written.
	How are their volumes fallen!

| Keeper | Only one! |

Jonah	Hold on there. Leave that open where it lies.
	Be careful not to lose the place. Be careful.
	Please let me have it.

| Jesse Bel | Read us what it says. |

| Jonah | Look, will you look! God can't put words in my mouth. |
| | My tongue's my own as True Thomas used to say. |

[17]

Keeper   So you've been Bohning up on Thomism too.

Jonah   Someone else read it.

Keeper   No, you read it to us.
And if it's prophecy, we'll see what happens.

Jonah   Nothing would happen. That's the thing of it.
God comes on me to doom a city for Him.
But oh no, not for Jonah. I refuse
To be the bearer of an empty threat.
He may be God, but me, I'm only human:
I shrink from being publicly let down.

Jesse Bel   Is this the love of God you preached to me?

Jonah   There's not the least lack of the love of God
In what I say. Don't be so silly, woman.
His very weakness for mankind's endearing.
I love and fear Him. Yes, but I fear for Him.
I don't see how it can be to His interest
This modern tendency I find in Him
To take the punishment out of all failure
To be strong, careful, thrifty, diligent,
Anything we once thought we had to be.

Keeper   You know what lets us off from being careful?

[18]

The thing that did what you consider mischief,
That ushered in this modern lenience
Was the discovery of fire insurance.
The future state is springing even now
From the discovery that loss from failure
By being spread out over everybody
Can be made negligible.

Paul   What's your book?
What's this?

Jonah   Don't lose the place.

Paul   Old Dana Lyle
Who reconciled the Pentateuch with science.

Jonah   Where shall I start in? Where my eyes fell first?
It seems to be a chapter head in meter.

Jesse Bel   It's too big for him. Help him hold it up.

Jonah   Someone else read it.

Keeper   No, you asked for it.

Jesse Bel   Come on, or we'll begin to be afraid.

Jonah   Well, but remember this is unofficial.

"The city's grotesque iron skeletons
Would knock their drunken penthouse heads together
And cake their concrete dirt off in the streets."
Then further down it seems to start from where
The city is admittedly an evil:
"O city on insecure rock pedestal,
So knowing—and yet needing to be told
The thought that added cubits to your height
Would better have been taken to your depth."
(*A whole shelf cascades down*) Here come some more.
The folly crashes and the dust goes up.

(*When the dust settles it should be apparent
Something has altered in the outer door*)

Jesse Bel   Mercy, for mercy's sake!

Keeper   Bel wants some mercy.
Kneel to your doctor. He dispenses mercy.
You're working it, old man. Don't be discouraged.

Jonah   This isn't it. I haven't prophesied.
This is God at me in my skulking place
Trying to flush me out. That's all it is.

Keeper   It's nothing but the Lending Library.
All secondhand. Don't get excited, folks,

[20]

The one indecency's to make a fuss
About our own or anybody's end.

Jonah   It's nothing I brought on by words of mine.

Keeper   You know there may have been a small temblor.
If so, it will be in tomorrow's paper.

Paul   Now if we've had enough of sacrilege,
We can go back to where we started from.
Let me repeat: I'm glad to hear you say
You can't trust God to be unmerciful.
What would you have God if not merciful?

Jonah   Just, I would have Him just before all else,
To see that the fair fight is really fair.
Then he could enter on the stricken field
After the fight's so definitely done
There can be no disputing who has won—
Then he could enter on the stricken field
As Red Cross Ambulance Commander in Chief
To ease the more extremely wounded out
And mend the others up to go again.

Paul   I thought as much. You have it all arranged,
Only to see it shattered every day.
You should be an authority on Mercy.

[21]

That book of yours in the Old Testament
Is the first place in literature I think
Where Mercy is explicitly the subject.
I say you should be proud of having beaten
The Gospels to it. After doing Justice justice,
Milton's pentameters go on to say,
But Mercy first and last shall brightest shine,
Not only last, but first, you will observe;
Which spoils your figure of the ambulance.

Keeper Paul only means you make too much of justice.
There's some such thing and no one will deny it—
Enough to bait the trap of the ideal
From which there can be no escape for us
But by our biting off our adolescence
And leaving it behind us in the trap.

Jonah Listen ye! It's the proletariat!
A revolution's coming down the street!
Light's out, I say, so's to escape attention.

(He snaps one bulb off. Paul snaps on another)

Jesse Bel You needn't shout like that, you wretched man.
There's nothing coming on us, is there, Paul?
We've had about enough of these sensations.
It's a coincidence, but we were on

[22]

The subject of the workers' revolution
When you came in. We're revolutionists.
Or Keeper is a revolutionist.
Paul almost had poor Keeper in a corner
Where he would have to quit his politics
Or be a Christian. Paul, I wish you'd say
That over. I shall have to retail it
To some of Keeper's friends that come in here,
A bunch of smalltime revolutionaries.
Paul makes it come out so they look like Christians.
How they'll like that. Paul said conservatives—
You say it, Paul.

Paul   You mean about success,
And how by its own logic it concentrates
All wealth and power in too few hands?
The rich in seeing nothing but injustice
In their impoverishment by revolution
Are right. But 'twas intentional injustice.
It was their justice being mercy-crossed.
The revolution Keeper's bringing on
Is nothing but an outbreak of mass mercy,
Too long pent up in rigorous convention—
A holy impulse towards redistribution.
To set out to homogenize mankind
So that the cream could never rise again.
Required someone who laughingly could play

[23]

With the idea of justice in the courts,
Could mock at riches in the right it claims
To count on justice to be merely just.
But we are talking over Jonah's head,
Or clear off what we know his interests are.
Still not so far off come to think of it.
There is some justice even as Keeper says.
The thing that really counts though is the form
Of outrage—violence—that breaks across it.
The very sleep we sleep is an example.
So that because we're always starting fresh
The best minds are the best at premises.
And the most sacred thing of all's abruption.
And if you've got to see your justice crossed
(And you've got to) which will you prefer
To see it, evil-crossed or mercy-crossed?

Keeper   We poets offer you another: star-crossed,
Of star-crossed, mercy-crossed, or evil-crossed
I choose the star-crossed as a star-crossed lover.

Jonah   I think my trouble's with the crisises
Where mercy-crossed to me seemed evil-crossed.

Keeper   Good for you Jonah. That's what I've been saying.
For instance when to purify the Itzas
They took my love and threw her down a well.

Jesse Bel	If it is me in my last incarnation
	He's thinking of, it wasn't down a well
	But in a butt of malmsey I was drowned.
Jonah	Why do you call yourself a star-crossed lover?
Keeper	Not everything I say is said in scorn.
	Some people want you not to understand them,
	But I want you to understand me wrong.
Jonah	I noticed how he just now made you out
	A revolutionary—which of course you can't be.
Keeper	Or not at least the ordinary kind.
	No revolution I brought on would aim
	At anything but change of personnel.
	The Andrew Jackson slogan of Vae Victis
	Or "Turn the rascals out" would do for me.
Paul	Don't you be made feel small by all this posing.
	Both of them caught it from Bel's favorite poet
	Who in his favorite pose as poet thinker
	(His was the doctrine of the Seven Poses)
	Once charged the Nazarene with having brought
	A darkness out of Asia that had crossed
	Old Attic grace and Spartan discipline
	With violence. The Greeks were hardly strangers

[25]

To the idea of violence. It flourished
Persisting from old Chaos in their myth
To embroil the very gods about their spheres
Of influence. It's been a commonplace
Ever since Alexander Greeced the world.
'Twere nothing new if that were all Christ brought.
Christ came to introduce a break with logic
That made all other outrage seem as child's play:
The Mercy on the Sin against the Sermon.
Strange no one ever thought of it before Him.
'Twas lovely and its origin was love.

Keeper   We know what's coming now.

Paul   You say it, Keeper,
If you have learned your lesson. Don't be bashful.

Keeper   Paul's constant theme. The Sermon on the Mount
Is just a frame-up to insure the failure
Of all of us, so all of us will be
Thrown prostrate at the Mercy Seat for Mercy.

Jesse Bel   Yes, Paul, you do say things like that sometimes.

Paul   You all have read the Sermon on the Mount.
I ask you all to read it once again.

*(They put their hands together like a book
And hold it up nearsightedly to read)*

Keeper and
Jesse Bel   We're reading it.

Paul   Well now you've got it read,
            What do you make of it?

Jesse Bel   The same old nothing.

Keeper   A beautiful impossibility.

Paul   Keeper, I'm glad you think it beautiful.

Keeper   An irresistible impossibility.
         A lofty beauty no one can live up to
         Yet no one turn from trying to live up to.

Paul   Yes, spoken so we can't live up to it
       Yet so we'll have to weep because we can't.
       Mercy is only to the undeserving.
       But such we all are made in the sight of God.
         "Oh what is a king here,
            And what is a boor?
            Here all starve together.
            All dwarfed and poor."

[27]

Here we all fail together, dwarfed and poor.

Failure is failure, but success is failure.

There is no better way of having it.

An end you can't by any means achieve

And yet can't turn your back on or ignore,

That is the mystery you must accept.

Do you accept it, Master Jonas Dove?

Jonah   What do you say to it, My Brother's Keeper?

Keeper   I say I'd rather be lost in the woods

Than found in church.

Jonah   That doesn't help me much.

Keeper   Our disagreement when we disagree, Paul,

Lies in our different approach to Christ,

Yours more through Rome, mine more through Palestine.

But let's be serious about Paul's offer.

His irresistible impossibility

His lofty beauty no one can live up to

Yet no one turn away from or ignore—

I simply turn away from it.

Paul   You Pagan!

Keeper   Yes, call me Pagan, Paul, as if you meant it.
I won't deceive myself about success
By making failure out of equal value.
Any equality they may exhibit's
In making fools of people equally.

Paul   But you—what is your answer, Jonas Dove?

Jonah   You ask if I see yonder shining gate,
And I reply I almost think I do,
Beyond this great door you have locked against me,
Beyond the storm, beyond the universe.

Paul   Yes, Pilgrim now instead of runaway,
Your fugitive escape become a quest.

Keeper   Don't let him make you see too bright a gate
Or you will come to with a foolish feeling.
When a great tide of argument sweeps in
My small fresh water spring gets drowned of course.
But when the brine goes back as go it must
I can count on my source to spring again
Not even brackish from its salt experience.
No true source can be poisoned.

Jonah   Then that's all.
You've finished. I'm dismissed. I want to run

[29]

Toward what you make me see beyond the world.
Unlock the door for me.

Keeper   Not that way out.

Jonah   I'm all turned round.

Paul   There is your way prepared.

Jonah   That's not my door.

Keeper   No, that's another door
Your exit door's become a cellar door.

(*The door here opens darkly of itself*)

Jonah   You mean I'm being sent down in the cellar?

Paul   You must make your descent like everyone.

Keeper   Go if you're going.

Jonah   Who is sending me?
Whose cellar is it, yours or the apostle's?

Keeper   It is the cellar to my store. What ho, down there!
My dungeoneers, come fetch us.—No one answers.

There's not much we can do till Martin gets here.—
Don't let me scare you. I was only teasing.
It is the cellar to my store, but not my cellar.
Jesse has given Paul the rent of it
To base his campaign on to save the world.

Jesse Bel Something's the matter everyone admits.
On the off-chance it may be lack of faith
I have contributed the empty cellar
To Paul to see what he can do with it
To bring faith back. I'm only languidly
Inclined to hope for much. Still what we need
Is something to believe in, don't we, Paul?

Keeper By something to believe in Jesse means
Something to be fanatical about
So as to justify the orthodox
In saving heretics by slaying them,
Not on the battlefield, but down in cellars.
That way's been tried too many times for me.
I'd like to see the world tried once without it.

Jesse Bel The world seems crying out for a Messiah.

Keeper Haven't you heard the news? We already have one,
And of the Messianic race, Karl Marx.

[31]

Jesse Bel   Light, bring a light!

Keeper   Awh, there's no lack of light, you—
A light that falls diffused over my shoulder
And is reflected from the printed page
And bed of world-flowers so as not to blind me.
If even the face of man's too bright a light
To look at long directly (like the sun),
Then how much more the face of truth must be.
We were not given eyes or intellect
For all the light at once the source of light—
For wisdom that can have no counterwisdom.
In our subscription to the sentiment
Of one God we provide He shall be one
Who can be many Gods to many men,
His church on earth a Roman Pantheon;
Which is our greatest hope of rest from war.
Live and let live, believe and let believe.
'Twas said the lesser gods were only traits
Of the one awful God. Just so the saints
Are God's white light refracted into colors.

Jesse Bel   Let's change the subject, boys, I'm getting nervous.

Keeper   Nervous is all the great things ever made you.
But to repeat and get it through your head:
We have all the belief that's good for us.

Too much all-fired belief and we'd be back
Down burning skeptics in the cellar furnace
Like Shadrac, Meshach, and Abednego.

Jonah   What's all this talk of slaying down in cellars—
So sinister? You spoke to someone down there.

Keeper   My friends and stokers, Jeffers and O'Neil.
They fail me. Now I'm teasing you again.
There's no one down there getting tortured save
A penitent perhaps self-thrown on Mercy.

Jonah   I heard a deep groan—maybe out of him.
What's really down there?

Paul   Just an oubliette,
Where you must lie in self-forgetfulness
On the wet flags before a crucifix
I have had painted on the cellar wall
By a religious Aztec Indian.

Jonah   Then it's not lethal—to get rid of me?
Have they been down?

Paul   Not in the proper spirit.
These two are stubborn children as you see.
Their case is not so simple. You are good.

[33]

Jonah   I am your convert. Tell me what I think.

My trouble has been with my sense of justice.

And you say justice doesn't really matter.

Paul   Does it to you as greatly as it did?

Jonah   I own the need of it had somewhat faded

Even before I came in here tonight.

Paul   Well then!

Jonah   And that's what I'm to meditate?

Paul   Meditate nothing. Learn to contemplate.

Contemplate glory. There will be a light.

Contemplate Truth until it burns your eyes out.

Jonah   I don't see any staircase.

Keeper   There are stairs.

Paul   Some lingering objection holds you back.

Jonah   If what you say is true, if winning ranks

The same with God as losing, how explain

Our making all this effort mortals make?

[34]

Keeper   Good for you, Jonah. That's what I've been saying.

Jonah   You'll tell me sometime. All you say has greatness.
Yet your friend here can't be quite disregarded.

Keeper   I say we keep him till we wring some more
Naïveness about Justice out of him,
As once the Pharoah did it out of Sekhti
By having him whipped every day afresh
For clamoring for justice at the gate
Until the scribes had taken down a bookful
For distribution to his bureaucrats.

Jonah   I'm going now. But don't you push me off.

Keeper   I was supporting you for fear you'd faint
From disillusionment. You've had to take it.

*(Jonah steps on the threshold as the door
Slams in his face. The blow and the repulse
Crumple him on the floor. Keeper and Paul
Kneel by him. Bel stands up beside her chair
As if to come, but Keeper waves her off)*

Jonah   I think I may have got God wrong entirely.

Keeper   All of us get each other pretty wrong.

Jesse Bel   Now we have done it, Paul. What did he say?

[35]

Jonah   I should have warned you, though my sense of justice
Was about all there ever was to me.
When that fades I fade—every time I fade.
Mercy on me for having thought I knew.

Jesse Bel   What did he say? I can't hear what he says.

Paul   Mercy on him for having asked for justice.

Keeper   Die saying that, old-fashioned sapient,
You poor old sape, if I may coin the slang.
We like you, don't we, Paul? (*Paul takes his wrist*)

Jesse Bel   (*Still standing off*) We've all grown fond of you.

Paul   We've all grown fond of you. (*Paul says it louder,
But Jonah gives no sign of having heard*)

Keeper   Who said too late you cannot enter now?

Jesse Bel   He was rejected for his reservations!

Keeper   (*Still on his knees he sits back on his heels*)
But one thing more before the curtain falls.
(*The curtain starts to fall*) Please hold the curtain—
All Paul means and I wish the dead could hear me,
All you mean Paul, I think—

[36]

Jesse Bel	Will you stand there
	And let that tell you what you think like that?

Paul	Suffer a friend to try to word you better.

Jesse Bel	Oh, there's to be a funeral oration.
	And we're an orator. Get up. Stand up
	For what you think your doctor thinks, why don't you?
	Don't wear your pants out preaching on your knees.
	Save them to say your prayers on.—What's the matter?

Keeper	(*He doesn't rise, but looks at her a moment*)
	Lady, at such a time, and in the Presence!
	I won't presume to tell Bel where to go.
	But if this prophet's mantle fell on me
	I should dare say she would be taken care of.
	We send our wicked enemies to Hell,
	Our wicked friends we send to Purgatory.
	But Bel gets some things right—and she was right—

Jesse Bel	(*She startles at the sudden note of kindness*)
	I *am* right then?

Keeper	In glorifying courage.
	Courage is of the heart by derivation,
	And great it is. But fear is of the soul.

[37]

And I'm afraid. (*The bulb lights sicken down.*
The cellar door swings wide and slams again)

Paul   The fear that you're afraid with is the fear
       Of God's decision lastly on your deeds.
       That is the Fear of God whereof 'tis written.

Keeper   But not the fear of punishment for sin
         (I have to sin to prove it isn't that),
         I'm no more governed by the fear of Hell
         Than by the fear of the asylum, jail, or poorhouse,
         The basic three the state is founded on.
         But I'm too much afraid of God to claim
         I have been fighting on the angels' side.
         That is for Him and not for me to say.
         For me to say it would be irreligious.
         (Sometimes I think you are too sure you have been.)
         And I can see that the uncertainty
         In which we act is a severity,
         A cruelty, amounting to injustice
         That nothing but God's mercy can assuage.
         I can see that, if that is what you mean.
         Give me a hand up, if we are agreed.

Paul   Yes, there you have it at the root of things.
       We have to stay afraid deep in our souls
       Our sacrifice, the best we have to offer,

[38]

And not our worst nor second best, our best,
Our very best, our lives laid down like Jonah's,
Our lives laid down in war and peace, may not
Be found acceptable in Heaven's sight.
And that they may be is the only prayer
Worth praying. May my sacrifice
Be found acceptable in Heaven's sight.

Keeper   Let the lost millions pray it in the dark!
My failure is no different from Jonah's.
We both have lacked the courage in the heart
To overcome the fear within the soul
And go ahead to any accomplishment.
Courage is what it takes and takes the more of
Because the deeper fear is so eternal.
And if I say we lift him from the floor
And lay him where you ordered him to lie
Before the cross, it is from fellow feeling,
As if I asked for one more chance myself
To learn to say (*He moves to Jonah's feet*)
Nothing can make injustice just but mercy.

Curtain